RISKY BUSINESS

Overcoming Fear
and Mastering the Art
of Conflict Resolution

By Barbara Bannon
Human Resource Investments

Barbara Bannon | 918 299 5227
email: Barbara@humanresourceinvestments.com or hri@cox.net
www.humanresourceinvestments.com

Table of Contents

Approaches, and a New Paradigm About Conflict
Self-Awareness
Stages of Group Development
Stage 1: Forming – Infancy
Stage 2: Norming – Childhood
Stage 3: Storming – Adolescence
Stage 4: Re-Norming – Pre-Adulthood
Stage 5: Performing – Adulthood
Group Norms and Other Dynamics

The Skill of Listening
The Ability to be Assertive
The Skill of Self-Management
Perceptions - Self-Talk – Behaviors
Stop – Access – Redirect
Influence and Persuasion
Step One – Active Listening
Step Two – Winning a Hearing
Step Three – Work to a Common Solution
Feedback and Accountability
Empathy
Wrong Way
Better Way
Empathy Model
Re-framing
Questions
Open Questions
Closed Questions
Fact-Finding Questions
Feeling-Finding Questions
Leading Questions

Introduction

There is nothing more destructive to the well-being and effective functioning of a group of people than unresolved and misdirected conflict. We've all experienced or observed it before: an environment in which people were fighting with one another at the expense of the real goals and purpose of the organization or relationship. Unresolved conflict can manifest itself in a variety of ways ranging from symptoms that are passive and take the form of: a lack of input, people don't speak up in staff or other meetings, managers seem to be the only ones with the ideas, it's difficult to get feedback even when it's asked for directly. Additionally, it can take more aggressive and obvious forms such as: gossip, inappropriate competition, backbiting or undermining. There is very little direct conversation and if it is direct it is brutal and ineffective in terms of providing real enlightenment or problem solving.

The inability to recognize and address conflict effectively, no matter how it manifests itself, makes it impossible to develop the kind of trusting and mature

1

relationships that contribute to the overall productivity of the organization. Why do people choose behaviors that get in the way of getting what they really want? Like most people, I didn't have a clue about the significance of conflict in my life and how it can affect the quality of both my personal and professional well-being until a couple of incidents occurred, which I will never forget and for which I will always be appreciative.

The first incident was what some people might refer to as one of those special gifts that come to you in the most unexpected and sometimes odd or unpleasant ways. Back around 1979 (I'm not good with exact dates) I had one of those uncomfortable experiences —you know—a learning experience. My boss told me that one of my co-workers had an issue with me and that we needed to go through a conflict resolution session. I was completely surprised. I didn't realize there was an issue between this co-worker and me. I did, however, agree to go through the session. I rarely turn down the opportunity for a new experience.

That experience, in which I had to deal directly with a conflict, turned out to be a genuine gift. What I learned was that conflict didn't have to end in the loss of a relationship. As a matter of fact, conflict, if dealt with effectively, can lead to stronger and deeper relationships.

The second incident occurred when I was in a workshop entitled; "The Managerial Grid" sponsored by the company for which I worked. The Grid was a wonderful tool for helping people understand and practice real teamwork. The workshop design consisted of many exercises requiring group problem-solving. We would do an exercise and then "process" what had happened and determine how to make the outcome more effective, by changing both processes and behaviors. As we were doing one of the exercises, one of the men in my group mentioned that "conflict is the real problem; we need to learn how to deal with conflict." I asked him, "Conflict about what?" At that time I didn't understand the significance of his observation. I discovered, after working with people as a Human Resource professional and as a manager, he was absolutely correct. The biggest problem associated with any human interaction is the inability to effectively resolve conflict over just about any issue.

The biggest problem associated with any human interaction is the inability to effectively resolve conflict.

These particular experiences with conflict led me to decide to study and even develop programs and materials to help others and me learn how to use conflict as a positive force in our lives. Over the last 25 years I have continued to develop materials for training and consulting in the area of conflict management and mediation.

In my years of working with people in organizational and court-mandated settings, I've observed that one of the biggest issues facing individuals in virtually all aspects of their lives, is the inability to address conflict effectively. I've seen that an individual's inability to address conflict leads to: decreased job performance and satisfaction, increased stress, and a decrease in the overall quality of life. For an organization, it can lead to reduced loyalty, higher turnover, lack or loss of trust, decreased teamwork, productivity and, of course, profit.

Most people aren't aware of the adverse impact on the organization created by the lack of conflict management skills. Those who are aware are only vaguely aware of exactly what this deficit can lead to, and generally have little or no understanding of how to overcome it.

Most people aren't aware of the adverse impact on the organization created by the lack of conflict management skills.

For me, the greatest benefits of learning how to

manage conflict more effectively include developing deeper, more loving, and non-defensive relationships with significant people in my life and helping others in the workplace resolve conflicts, thereby minimizing stress and enhancing satisfaction.

It isn't necessary to be a psychologist to facilitate a resolution to conflict.

It isn't necessary to be a psychologist to facilitate a resolution to conflict. It is, however, important to develop some of the fundamental skills and qualities I've outlined in the text of this book.

I've written this book in a very informal style because that is the style with which I feel most comfortable. Additionally, you will find that I often introduce important issues by raising them as a question directed to you, the reader, and to me as if I were being interviewed. This approach complements my informal style and I hope provides an aid to you in understanding the topic.

I believe you will find the information useful in helping you identify and develop the skills that can assist in addressing conflict more effectively. I also believe that the awareness and development of these skills can help reduce stress and lead to more enjoyment in both your business and personal life.

Purpose

The purpose of this book is to stimulate thoughts, provide information and act as a reference guide for individuals who want to learn more about the dynamics and benefits associated with conflict. Additionally, it is a refresher and support document for those who have attended the sessions I conduct on 'communication and conflict management.' The book is divided into sections. Each section addresses a different aspect of conflict.

Section One of the book addresses in considerable detail the concept of conflict management, what happens when conflict isn't managed effectively, and why we tend to avoid addressing conflict.

Section Two deals with "where to start", which includes self-awareness and group dynamics.

Section Three deals with the fundamental skills it takes to communicate more effectively in order to begin to manage conflict.

Section Four covers common communication barriers. These are words and phrases, which can get in the way of any communication process by creating or escalating a conflict. Awareness of these barriers can assist you in recognizing and avoiding the use of such expressions.

Section Five presents several models for addressing conflict and problem solving.

Section Six is the closing section in which I present some final thoughts about making the changes it will take to be more effective in addressing conflict.

Section Seven is biographical information about me, the author of "Risky Business," Barbara Bannon.

Section One

The Concept of Conflict and Its Effects

Lack of awareness of the symptoms of unresolved conflict can lead to reduced profitability, diminished creativity, decreased loyalty and worker satisfaction, generally making your organization less attractive to healthy people. If these observations concern you, you need to understand the connection between unresolved conflict and poor performance. The manifestations of unresolved conflict are quite common in most business (and personal) relationships.

More often than not the symptoms go undiagnosed, unaddressed and unresolved. When that is reversed and conflict is diagnosed and addressed effectively, it can lead to greater trust, which can lead to greater economic efficiencies and personal gratification. Even though most people can describe the benefits of

Lack of awareness of the symptoms of unresolved conflict can lead to reduced profitability, diminished creativity, decreased loyalty and worker satisfaction.

Greater trust, can lead to greater economic efficiencies and personal gratification.

7

being in an environment in which conflict is resolved, they still don't make the connection between the symptoms of unresolved conflict and the real and everyday problems they deal with as a result. If this connection were clearly understood, far more attention would be given to help people learn to better address conflict.

As a matter of fact, many business people will deny that conflict even exists in their organization. I believe such denial stems primarily from an inability to recognize the symptoms of unresolved conflict and not from intentional negligence.

Most people define conflict so narrowly that they certainly wouldn't, and probably don't, have such behavior present in their environments. For most people the word conflict connotes fighting, tension, unhappiness, ugliness or even violence of some type. For example, I was invited by the president of a company to discuss with him and his vice presidents what they might need to create a more effective and productive environment. I happened to know there was a great deal of dysfunctional behavior related to unresolved conflict such as territorial behaviors, undermining efforts, talking about one another rather than to one another, and creating competitive situations where competition wasted resources. So, when the president asked me what type of development effort could be most beneficial for his organization, I said "conflict management."

He looked at me and said that there wasn't any conflict in his organization. I thought he was joking so I started laughing. When I looked around the table and saw none of the VPs laughing, I realized he was serious. I quickly responded by saying, "Well we are probably defining conflict differently; to me conflict is a clashing of ideas, and if there isn't any conflict in an environment, then there isn't any creativity." He paused for a moment and said, "When you put it that way we

Conflict is a clashing of ideas, and if there isn't any conflict in an environment, then there isn't any creativity.

probably do have conflict." If there isn't any conflict there isn't any passion either, and nothing could be worse for any work environment or relationship than to be passionless.

Helping people move away from the belief that conflict is bad, unproductive and undesirable is an important step in freeing people to use conflict as a means of positive energy in their lives. When we look at conflict as a clash of ideas, the expression of needs and creativity, of passion and commitment, it is easier to acknowledge and confront. Conflict is not bad! What is bad is the damage that is done when conflict isn't properly or effectively addressed. So why isn't it addressed? I believe there are three primary reasons: (1) it is not recognized, (2) people don't know how to respond to it, (3) there is too much fear or lack of desire to resolve it.

Okay, so you can accept that people might not recognize or know how to address conflict, but why would people lack the desire to address it? People can lack desire for a variety of reasons, many of which I'm qualified to comment on simply from experience; other reasons are better left to psychologists and counselors.

Some of the reasons people may lack desire are:

- They don't understand the benefits that can accrue for the organization or their relationships if they learn to confront.
- They are too disillusioned and uncommitted to the relationship or organization to expend the energy needed to resolve the conflict.
- They're afraid, fear keeps them from trying.
- They have an addiction to, or a need to be in constant conflict or ineffective relationships.
- They withhold or use lack of response as a form of control/power.

If there isn't any conflict - there isn't any passion either, and nothing could be worse for any work environment or relationship than to be passionless.

Conflict is not bad!

- They don't know how, and don't have the resources or motivation to learn how.
- They view the risk as too great with little reward.

It takes desire, demonstrated by commitment to the process, as well as the necessary skills to resolve conflict.

Whatever the reason for a lack of desire, it means that conflict cannot be resolved. It takes desire, demonstrated by commitment to the process, as well as the necessary skills to resolve conflict.

Managing or confronting conflict is never easy, but it can be much less difficult if individuals develop the appropriate skills. Communication style also influences our initial response to conflict. Once we become aware of our basic beliefs about conflict and our initial "most comfortable response" to conflict, we can then make a conscious decision as to how we want to address it.

We don't really manage conflict - we manage ourselves. Developing self-management skills allows us to respond to a situation versus react.

The term managing conflict is really a misnomer. We don't really manage conflict - we manage ourselves. Developing self-management skills allows us to respond to a situation versus react. Surely self-management isn't the only skill needed to effectively influence the outcome of a conflict? Correct - it isn't. Self-management is actually a very important set of skills related to dealing with conflict. Additionally, self-management is no small task to accomplish. If it were, you wouldn't be reading this book.

I believe the types of skills and characteristics it takes to deal effectively with conflict are:

Important Skills & Characteristics for Resolving Conflict
- listening
- observation
- empathy
- objectivity
- assertiveness
- the ability to center on another's needs
- facilitation
- speaking in specifics
- negotiation

- problem solving
- self awareness
- self talk awareness
- knowledge of words
  and behaviors that can cause defensiveness
- open mindedness
- giving feedback
- using descriptive language
- process management

This all sounds like a pretty simple cause-and-effect relationship between compromised results and the ability to manage conflict, so why do people continue to behave in ways that don't produce better results? Why do people repeat the same behaviors thinking they are going to get different outcomes? These are very good questions and often when we ask these questions about the behavior of a peer or boss (or client), it's with disbelief and sometimes disdain for their lack of willingness.

One of the key concepts I keep in mind to help me be more supportive and tolerant of people caught in these old and dysfunctional patterns of behavior is the knowledge that, "most people would do better if they knew how." If I accept the above stated belief, it's much easier for me to work with and support a change in another individual's behavior than if I believe that person "just isn't trying" or "they prefer this behavior."

Most people would do better if they knew how.

Can all of us be highly effective at resolving conflict? Like anything else, some of us are going to be better at some things than others. The same is true with regard to confronting conflict. However, if you have the desire to improve and focus on developing the skills it takes to be better, anyone can improve.

Section Two

Where to Start?
Approaches, and a
New Paradigm About Conflict

Next we'll examine both the approaches we tend to use in dealing with conflict and then we'll begin to examine ourselves and the characteristics of group dynamics which influence human behavior.

I believe there are three primary approaches to dealing with conflict:

        1) avoidance
        2) react/control
        3) confront/manage

Using judgment to decide momentarily—not to respond hastily in any given situation—is different from avoidance. It becomes avoidance when it goes beyond momentary, when there is resulting unfinished business, lack of closure or personal dissatisfaction with the outcome of the encounter.

Rationalizing avoidance is easy to do! There are so many seemingly good reasons for avoiding confrontation, such as, "the timing just wasn't right," "it might hurt their feelings," "it's probably just a misunderstanding" etc. etc. etc. When does a reason become an excuse? When we use that reason to abdicate responsibility for achieving the best possible results.

Listed below are criteria against which you can measure behaviors and characteristics in order to assess which approach you generally use in dealing with conflict:

Avoidance	React/control	Confront/manage
• Indirect (suggestive)	• Aggressive	• Assertive
• Passive	• Combative	• Descriptive
• Indifferent	• Punitive	• Solution Centered
• Minimizing	• Defensive	• Empathetic
• Victim of Circumstances	• Accusatory (blaming)	• Seek Cause
• Lacks confidence	• Minimizing	• Provisional
	• Demanding	• Supportive
	• Judging	• Self-confident
	• Lacks confidence	

Below are some broad statements describing the behaviors and results associated with each of these approaches to dealing with conflict. After you have read through them, try to determine which approach/es you tend to use most frequently.

Using judgment to decide momentarily, not to respond hastily in any given situation, is different from avoidance.

Rationalizing avoidance is easy to do!

When does a reason become an excuse? When we use that reason to abdicate responsibility for achieving the best possible results.

Avoiding: generally unassertive and uncooperative. An individual doesn't immediately pursue his/her own concerns or those of the other person. He/she doesn't address the conflict. Avoiding might take the form of diplomatically sidestepping an issue, postponing an issue until a better time, or simply withdrawing from a situation which is perceived as threatening.

Reacting/Controlling: aggressive and uncooperative. An individual pursues his/her own concerns at the other person or group's expense. This is a power-oriented mode, in which one uses whatever power seems appropriate to win one's position, including one's ability to argue, one's rank, economic status. These actions usually lead to short-term wins and long-term losses.

Confronting/Managing: both assertive and cooperative. The opposite of avoiding. Confronting/managing involves an attempt to work with the other person/s to arrive at a solution which fully satisfies the concerns of both/all parties. It means:
- digging into an issue to identify the underlying concerns of the two individuals and to find an alternative which meets both persons' concerns.
- collaborating
- problem solving between two or more persons that might take the form of exploring a disagreement to learn from each other's insights,
- concluding to resolve some condition which would otherwise have them competing for resources, or
- confronting and trying to find a creative solution to an interpersonal problem.

Effective confrontation isn't easy. Nothing that requires a change in behavior is easy.

Understanding the benefits and downsides to these approaches is a key motivator in choosing to confront and manage conflict. Effective confrontation isn't easy. Nothing that requires a change in behavior is easy. The fears associated with past experiences in confrontation get in the way of trying again—and rightfully so—if one hasn't learned any new skills for confronting. Another impediment is all the "old baggage" associated with the word confrontation or conflict.

Generally, people choose only negative words to describe conflict or confrontation. Since this is the case, it's critical to help people redefine and visualize a more positive paradigm for conflict and confrontation. In order to help people understand the effect conflict avoidance can have in a workplace, or home, I have and do ask hundreds of workshop participants the following questions:

"Recall a time when you were in an environment where conflict was dealt with through avoidance; what did it look and feel like? How did people behave and react and what were the results?" Based on their experiences, I get answers like these; frustration, resignation (literally and figuratively), little or no communication, cliques, people talking about each other versus with each other, rumors, indirect or suggestive communication, passive/aggressive behavior, low energy, little creativity or enthusiasm. Additionally, the results they've seen are; little teamwork, increased turnover, lack of commitment, mistakes, decreased productivity and job satisfaction, increased stress, and ultimately decreased profit.

When I ask the same questions in relation to being in an environment in which conflict is dealt with through a react/control response, many of the descriptors are the same, with the addition of; violence, anger, aggression, threats and intimidation. The work (or personal) results tend to be the same. So a lack of conflict management can greatly decrease the quality and desirability of the work environment, to say nothing of productivity and profitability.

Lack of conflict management can decrease greatly the quality and desirability of the work environment, to say nothing of productivity and profitability.

We've all experienced these effects and results. We may not have clearly associated them with a lack of conflict management skills but obviously, at some level, we are aware that avoidance and control can lead to these very ineffective outcomes.

Where to Start?
Self-Awareness

Next we'll concentrate on self-awareness, then on understanding the stages of group development, and finally, the importance of understanding and managing norms. If you have a better understanding of yourself, your "hot buttons," red flags, the things that cause you to react, you can be more effective at making choices about your own development. The kinds of questions you'll address in the process of becoming more self-aware with regard to conflict are:

- What predominant approach do I take in dealing with conflict and why?
- What are the characteristics of my style that are potential strengths in confronting conflict

and in what areas am I likely to need development?

- Why do I have the feelings I do in confrontational situations?
- What beliefs are associated with my behaviors?
- What behaviors and skills will I need in order to manage confrontation situations more effectively?

You don't have to know the answers to all of these self-assessment questions, but it's helpful to understand more about what causes you to react the way you do.

Do some people have more difficulty with self-awareness than others? Yes, and again, for a variety of reasons. In the past couple of decades there have been some relatively new developments in measuring intelligence. These new developments and directions are moving us away from the popularly held belief that intelligence can be measured only as it relates to verbal and mathematical or analytical skills. Research is uncovering the existence of multiple forms of intelligence. These multiple forms of intelligence include intra-personal intelligence or the capacity to assess and take stock of oneself—what I've been referring to as self-awareness. If this is true, and I believe from personal experience it is, some people will have a greater capacity for self-awareness than others. This, nonetheless, shouldn't be used as an excuse to avoid enhancing self-awareness.

Some people will have a greater capacity for self-awareness than others.

Awareness precedes choice; with greater self-awareness one has more choices regarding available behaviors and options. If I have no or limited awareness, I have no or limited choices. For example, I was working with a corporate Human Resource (H.R.) executive who had been having a lot of turnover in her department and several instances of passive/aggressive behavior toward her leadership. Some of this passive/-aggressive behavior took the form of missing deadlines

Awareness precedes choice; with greater self-awareness one has more choices regarding available behaviors and options.

or resisting taking initiative on important projects for which she had established completion dates. After speaking with her and her team members, and watching them interact, I met with her and told her (with her permission) I thought her behavior was intimidating to the people who reported to her, and additionally that they felt she didn't care to hear their input.

She was shocked and couldn't imagine why anyone would be intimidated. I helped her understand that even though her behaviors weren't meant to intimidate that they, in fact, did. I gave her several specific examples of the kind of behaviors that could be creating such an impression. We worked together to come up with some communication strategies that would work more effectively for both her and those who reported to her.

So how do you become aware? There are many methods you can use, singularly or jointly, ranging from the use of behavioral or style inventories, to third party feedback, as in the above situation. Another method for increasing awareness is self-assessment through requested feedback. One such method requires assessing yourself against a list of skills and personal characteristics you want to develop, like the ability to confront or resolve conflict. This list can then be used as criteria against which you can measure feedback from others. A combination of both self and other feedback is probably the most effective approach to increased self-awareness.

Additionally, in the last decade or so there has been more research and empirical evidence surfaced about the physiological differences between the brains of men and women with regard to communication and conflict. I'll list below some of the key concepts about those differences that I've found very helpful in understanding how we can often misinterpret one another, which can lead to unintended conflict. This information is provided so you can evaluate and consider how you might use it to benefit your organization or personal relationships. Please do additional reading on the subject of brain differences; it will be very enlightening and helpful for improved outcomes in both the workplace and home.

Fast Facts in Research Data on the Psychological Differences Between Men and Women's Brains

Because of some of the more current research on the physiological differences in men and women's brains, along with greater understanding of the affects of hormones on the brain, we—as business professionals and life partners—can respond more effectively amd appreciate the different strengths we bring to dealing with a variety of situations, including conflict. As food for thought and self-reflection, I've listed some of these findings below:

- There is 15 to 20% more blood flow in a women's brain than in a man's at any given time. Blood flow enables different parts of the brain to work simultaneously in ways that the male brain does not.
- The male brain shuts off (enters a rest state) many times per day, but the female brain does not shut down in the same way; as a result, women and men generally have different approaches to paying attention.
- Women take in more through each of their five senses than men do, on average, and store more of this material in the brain for later use. Thus they tend to remember more details during a conversation.
- When the male brain is angry, the swelling of the amygdala leads to a near closure of a lot of

the verbal circuits.
- Emotional processing and our approach to developing self-esteem and emotional intelligence is quite different in men and women especially because women's brains tend to link more of the emotional activity that is going on in the middle of the brain (the limbic system) with thoughts and words in the top of the brain (the cerebral cortex). Thus a man might need many hours to process a major emotion-laden experience, whereas a woman may be able to process it quite quickly.

Men and Women In Conflict

Men:
- Tend to become more physically dominant.
- Tend to curse more, especially with other men.
- Often distance themselves from conflict deciding the problem is external to them and they don't need to deal with it.

Women:
- Are more likely to feel it more and worry about how it is their fault versus how to solve it immediately.
- Are more likely to personalize it and store up anger for longer periods of time.

The above listed findings are a few which are addressed in a book entitled: "Leadership and the Sexes" by Michael Gurian and Barbara Annis.

Where to Start?
Stages of Group Development

After examining self-awareness, since conflict does-n't exist in a vacuum, we now need to gain a greater understanding of the natural stages of group development. I've included below a model developed many years ago by Richard Weber. My experience in working with groups led me to make some additions to this very effective model. I'll indicate my work by using italics. I've included this model because I found that being familiar with it helps managers and leaders understand certain behaviors we can expect at each stage of development of a work team (or couple), and with this understanding we can better address group or relationship needs.

You'll note below that the titles of each stage of

There are certain behaviors we can expect at each stage of development of a work team, and with this understanding we can better address group needs.

21

group development are associated with the stages of human physical development, I think you will understand why as you read through the descriptions.

Stage 1: Forming - Infancy
When a team is forming, members look for and explore the boundaries of acceptable group behavior. This is a stage of transition and decision-making—transitioning from individual status, and making decisions with regard to whether or not you really want to become part of this group or relationship. There's lack of clarity of the purpose, the individual's role in the group, along with mostly silent judgment/ evaluation of the role of leadership.

The Forming stage includes these types of behaviors:
   * Attempts to define tasks and how they will be accomplished.
   * Attempts to determine acceptable group behavior and how to deal with group problems.
   * Decisions on what information needs to be gathered and shared.
   * Discussion of symptoms or problems not relevant to the task; difficulty in identifying relevant problems.
   * Complaints about the organization (relationship) and the barriers that get in the way of accomplishing the task/s.

Stage 2: Norming - Childhood
During this stage, members accept the team, the stated and unstated team norms, and their roles in the team. Apparent conflict, because of this willingness to accept the status quo, is reduced. Team members may believe they can be more successful by going along.

The Norming Stage includes these behaviors:
   * Attempts to achieve harmony by avoiding con-

flict.
* More friendliness, confiding in each other, and
  sharing of personal problems; discussing the
  team's dynamics.
* The desire to create a sense of team cohe-
  sion, common spirit and goals.
* Attempts at establishing team ground rules
  and boundaries (norms).

Stage 3: Storming - Adolescence

Storming is probably the most difficult stage for the
team. Team members begin to realize the task is different and more difficult than they imagined. They
may become testy, blameful, or overzealous. The ten-
dency to go along is overcome by a sense of frustration related to suppressing real concerns.

Impatient about the lack of progress, but still too
inexperienced or unskilled, members will argue about
what actions the team should take. They try to rely
solely on their personal and professional experience,
resisting the need to collaborate with other team
members.

The Storming Stage includes these behaviors:
* Arguing among members even when they agree
  on the real issue.
* Defensiveness and competition; factions and
  "choosing sides."
* Questioning the wisdom of those who selected
  the other members of the team.
* Concern about excessive work.
* A perceived "pecking order"; disunity,
  increased tension, and jealousy.

Stage 4: Re-Norming - Pre-Adulthood
*This stage is one that occurs because of growing
awareness of the need, and subsequent effort, to
come together to identify and develop specific skills,*

behaviors (norms) and characteristics in order to advance to Stage 5.

The Re-Norming Stage includes the identification and development of the following skills and characteristics:
  * *Listening*
  * *Problem Solving*
  * *Process assessment and evaluation*
  * *Feedback (giving and receiving)*
  * *Self-management*
  * *Assertiveness*
  * *Facilitation*
  * *Honesty*
  * *Humor*
  * *Establishing common, clear and shared goals, norms and purpose.*

Stage 5: Performing - Adulthood
By this stage, the team has clarified its relationships and expectations. They can begin performing—diagnosing and solving problems, and choosing and implementing changes. At last team members have discovered and accepted each other's strengths and weaknesses, and learned their respective roles.

Performing includes these behaviors:
  * Constructive self-change.
  * Ability to prevent or work through group problems.
  * Close attachment to the team.

Where To Start?
Group Norms and
Other Dynamics

It's critical to understand that with the development

or reformation (change) of any team, or relationship, new norms are established. What are norms? Norms can be defined as a standard, binding upon members of the group and serving to guide, control or regulate behavior. A spoken or unspoken standard of conduct. Norms can be consciously established or can unconsciously surface in a group or any relationship.

Norms can have both a positive effect on the work group, business environment, or family or they can create tremendous barriers to effective teamwork and work products. Norms can affect the way work is done (or not), they can affect how people communicate, how they deal with or don't deal with conflict, whether or not performance issues are addressed, what's acceptable in terms of project quality, teamwork or work effort.

The leader or individual who doesn't consciously choose to establish and manage the norms in a team, or in a personal relationship, may become the victim of those norms—don't let this happen!

Additionally, a discussion of group process and dynamics wouldn't be complete without, at least, some mention of both the concept of group-think and the power of expectations, or the Pygmalion Effect.

Group-think is often explained through the use of a parable entitled; "The Road to Abilene." This is a story about a family who is sitting at home, relaxed, but slightly bored, when one of the members suggests that they make a trip to Abilene, which is several hours away. The rest of the family members passively agree to make the trip, thinking that the person who made the suggestion really wants to go. They arrive, after a long and fairly uneventful trip, at a restaurant in town, have an uninspired meal and return home. Upon returning home they start to dis-

Norms can be defined as a standard, binding upon members of the group and serving to guide, control or regulate behavior.

Norms can have both a positive effect on the work group or they can create tremendous barriers to effective teamwork and work products.

The leader or individual who doesn't consciously choose to establish and manage the norms in a team, or in a personal relationship, may become the victim of those norms.

cuss the trip and discover that they really didn't want to go to Abilene but because no one spoke up they ended up going along. This is a perfect example of group-think and it is also a perfect example of how the fear of confrontation and feedback can lead people in directions they don't really want to go, at home or in the workplace.

What we expect from one another is what we get from one another.

The Pygmalion Effect is about the power of expectations for both good and bad results. What we expect from one another is what we get from one another. The Pygmalion or Expectation Cycle is composed of four steps: 1) the formation of expectations of others; 2) our verbal or non-verbal communication of our expectations; 3) people respond to the cues by adjusting their behavior to our expectations; and 4) the expectation appears to miraculously come true.

There are four (4) specific areas in which we can consciously or unconsciously affect others: 1) climate: we create a positive or negative interpersonal climate; 2) input: we teach more to those with whom we expect more or less to those with whom we expect less; 3) the Output factor: when they ask, we give more or less; 4) the feedback factor: we tell them not only how well they've done but also how they could do better or we focus only on how poorly they have done.

The behaviors which affect climate are: tone, body language, eye contact and facial expression. These cues are subtle and we may be unaware of how they affect others. The amount and quality of input manifests itself through such behaviors as: providing challenging assignments to encourage individuals to expand skills or the opposite. We can affect results through output by how often we encourage people to speak and how well we listen and finally the kind of feedback we give others has a direct effect on their sense of self-worth and self-esteem.

Next we'll discuss several skills that are essential in effectively confronting and solving conflict, starting with the skill of listening.

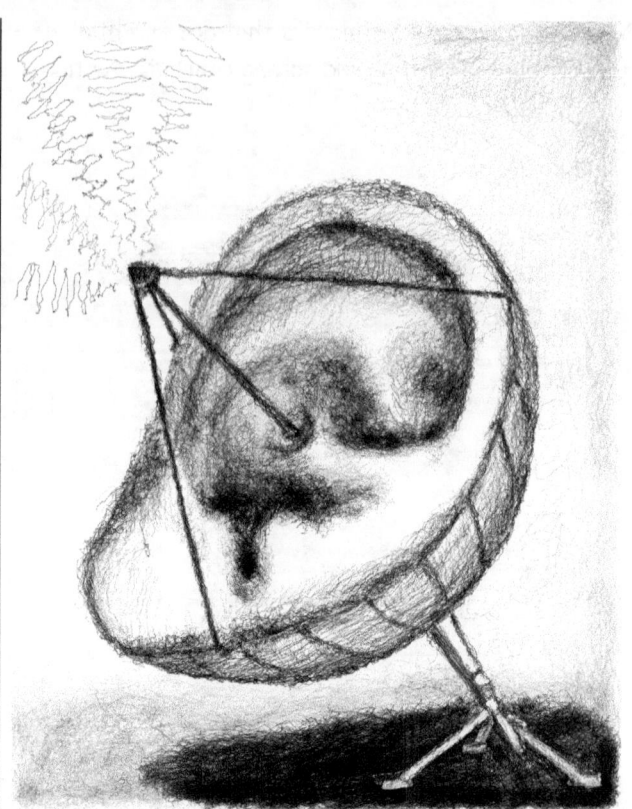

Section Three - Skills

The Skill of Listening

Listening is a way of showing respect for another human being. Conversely, a lack of listening is a way of showing disrespect.

Anytime I discuss the topic of listening in my workshops there is always agreement as to the great importance of this skill. One of the reasons it's so important is because listening is a way of showing respect for another human being. Conversely, a lack of listening is a way of showing disrespect. Listening is also one of our least developed skills. If we are all in agreement as to the importance and value of this skill, why don't we do it more and better?

It's been said that the reason people don't listen for understanding is because if they truly understood the other person's point of view they might have to change their mind ... and change creates fear. The implication then is that one of the biggest reasons for a lack of listening is fear. When I originally heard this statement I thought it a little far-fetched but, as I became more aware of my own behaviors and as I observed others, I found this to be true. People tended to fear such things as a loss of control or a loss of face, or the fear of hearing something they just didn't want to hear. *Thank you Carl Rogers for these insights about listening for understanding!*

Another reason listening is so difficult is because in order to truly understand another person, the listener has to center on the other person (be other-centered). Generally, we are very self-centered, so instead of focusing on how the speaker thinks and feels about what he/she is saying, we focus on how we think and feel about what the speaker is saying—we are self-centered. It's very difficult to break the habit of centering on self and it's impossible to break this habit if we don't have the awareness that we're doing this in the first place.

In order to truly understand another person, the listener has to be other-centered.

Listening can also be a means of influence or control, for better or worse. If the person being spoken to doesn't display listening behaviors when being addressed, the speaker may interpret that behavior as an insult, and then respond in a passive or aggressive fashion. The speaker may stop speaking or making contributions in the future, or may lash out through aggressive or even passive-aggressive behaviors.

Sometimes the lack of listening behavior can be an unconscious means of influencing the speaker's behavior. In other words, the person being spoken to isn't even aware that he/she is discouraging the speaker by her behavior. It can also be true that the person being spoken to does know what effect her behavior has on the speaker and is choosing this response very intentionally. If you've ever been irritated, or excited, and started to explain your situation to someone who wouldn't listen, you know how frustrating it can be.

In addition to listening for the facts in a communication exchange it is important to become sensitized to the more subtle messages such as:
- What the person is feeling (feelings).
- What the person is thinking (meaning).

Listening behavior can influence the productivity, creativity and the quality of interactions and outcomes in any relationship. It's a very valuable and powerful skill that requires a great deal of practice. Additionally, since the listener has no idea what the speaker may say, or how what the speaker says may affect him/her, listening also takes a great deal of self-confidence. The value added to any relationship from effective listening is immeasurable.

Listening behavior can influence the productivity, creativity and the quality of nteractions and outcomes in any relationship.

Listening also takes a great deal of self-confidence.

The Ability to be Assertive

One of the most common problems associated with

the inability to manage conflict is the lack of skills associated with being assertive. In most environments there's very little assertive behavior. Since the primary approach used in dealing with conflict is "to not deal with it," or avoidance, it follows that passive behavior or passive/aggressive behaviors are very common in most environments. Additionally, aggressive behavior is also quite common. Usually aggressive behavior occurs when people finally get so fed up with a situation that they react angrily.

There is a great deal of confusion about the difference between aggressive behavior and assertive behavior, and this confusion is complicated by the fact that aggression, like harassment, is judged from the eye of the beholder/target. For example, if I use assertive behavior and I'm dealing with someone who is quite passive or quite aggressive, my behavior can be viewed by him or her as aggressive. Sounds like a "Catch 22." Even though this complicates communication, you can reduce potential misinterpretation by being very aware that your behavior may be misinterpreted. It's important to watch for cues in the other person's behavior that suggest they may be misinterpreting your actions or words.

Like harassment, aggression is judged from the eye of the beholder.

Here's an example: you are the leader of a department. Your team is working on a problem and you offer an opinion about a possible approach for solving the problem. It isn't your intention for the team to give up its own ideas, but merely to express one in addition. You notice that after you speak, the energy in the room lowers and everyone is tentatively agreeing with you. You now have an opportunity to clarify your intentions to add one of many ideas to be considered, and encourage them to continue their own exploration.

So what are the elements of assertive behavior and communication? The first element is honesty. It's

The first element is honesty. It's impossible to have effective communication if you're not honest.

31

impossible to have effective communication if you're not honest. The biggest reason for a lack of honesty in communication is fear. Fear that we may hurt someone's feelings, fear of retaliation, etc. However, fear often gets much greater weight than it merits. I encourage you to face the fear, because with your new skills, you can learn to confront more effectively.

Often our honesty, or what we rationalize as honesty, is an attack on the other person. For example, the following statement might qualify as an attack: "You are such a control freak in these meetings." The speaker is obviously frustrated with someone's behavior and if the message is delivered in this manner, there probably will be an escalation of the problem. The key to effective confrontation is to refrain from using judgmental language such as name calling, and focus on the relevant and specific behavior that's causing you concern.

Assertive behavior will help clarify specific needs and offer specific, non-judgmental and constructive feedback, which will improve the chance of getting the desired results. For example, in the same situation as above, the speaker might say something like; "I feel 'put down' and as if you aren't interested in my ideas when you keep interrupting me in these meetings." This type of approach can leave room for the opportunity to discuss and resolve the real issues and concerns, and can move the encounter away from a possible escalation of defensive behaviors.

Another situation in which you might need to be assertive is when someone asks something of you that you don't really feel you can do. The issue is "how do I get what I need and at the same time meet the needs of the person making the request?" The first thing you have to determine in a situation like this is; (from your perspective) what is negotiable and what is not. Once you've determined what is possible and what is not, you then communicate first what you "can do" versus what you "can't do." Even if you can't do exactly what the person is requesting, let them know what you *can* do first.

The reason for focusing on what you "can do" is crucial because saying "no," first thing can break a psychological connection with the other party that you may not be able to recover. This is a simple concept and certainly sounds logical but it is rarely used. For example, a customer or co-worker asks: "Can you get this report to me by noon?" Your initial response, if it's a request you can't meet at that time, is often "no," which may or may not be followed by a statement of what you can do. By this time the speaker is focusing attention on how he/she feels about the "no" and is probably not willing to listen to the rest of the explanation.

Saying "no," first thing can break a psychological connection with the other party that you may not be able to recover.

In order to avoid breaking that connection, it's better to focus on 'what you "can do"' first. For example: "I can get that report to you by 2:00 p.m. How will that work?" Hearing "no" first establishes a defensive atmosphere we can easily avoid by saying first what we "can do." People don't come to you for what you can't do; they come for what you can do. We're in the habit, for a variety of reasons, of giving the bad news first. We can break that habit and it's well worth the effort to do so.

People don't come to you for what you can't do; they come for what you can do.

The third step in assertive behavior is to ensure your discussion is conducted in a manner that creates a sense of equality. Helping the party you're communicating with feel respected and equal is key to a positive outcome. The skills associated with this step are the ability to listen, ask appropriate questions, surface and address their needs as well as your own. In summary the three steps associated with assertive

The third step in assertive behavior is to ensure your discussion is conducted in a manner that creates a sense of equality.

behavior are:

1) be honest about what is relevant,

2) know what is possible and what is not, with emphasis on what you "can do,"

3) treat the other party as an equal.

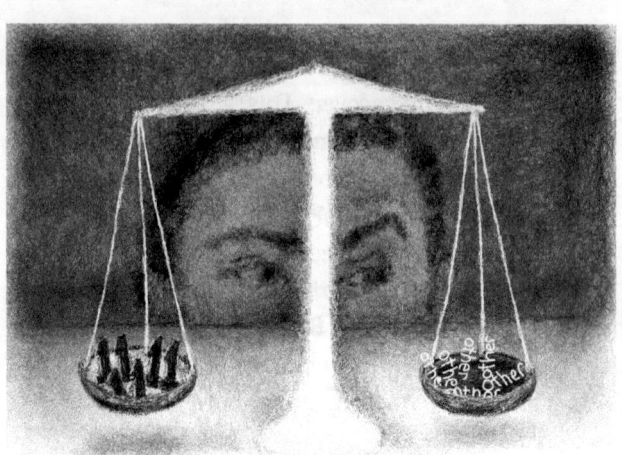

The Skill of Self-Management

In any encounter there's potential for conflict. When you're confronted, you have choices. You can choose to react hastily, attack, be passive, or respond and be assertive. The process of self-management assists you in using what you know to respond appropriately rather than react hastily. Keep in mind, you have no control over anyone else! You can't control the way another person behaves toward you, but you can influence his or her behavior through your own. The only real control is self-control.

The only real control is self-control.

We talk to ourselves all day long, every day. In order to be as effective as we can in dealing with conflict, we must become aware of the messages we're sending ourselves, so we can use those messages to influence

the outcomes of our encounters. How do you influence the outcomes of encounters? Initially through
self-talk, we all come to every encounter with one or
more perceptions or misperceptions. Those perceptions lead to self-talk which influences our behavior.

*Those percep-
tions lead to self-
talk which influ-
ence our behavior.*

Perceptions · Self-Talk · Behaviors

Say for example, based on my past experiences, I've
developed a particularly negative perception of male
bosses. Based on that perception, prior to meeting my
new male boss, my self-talk might be something like
this: "I can't believe I've got to put up with another
male boss. They just don't communicate very effectively, their sense of empathy is low, and I don't know
how I'm going to suffer through this." If that is the
kind of self-talk going on in my head, what types of
behavior might I display? Possibly standoffish,
closed, aloof or curt? Perception leads to self-talk,
which leads to behavior.

The awareness of perceptions and self-talk is particularly critical when you're faced with a situation of
potential conflict. Imagine you have someone walk into
your office and accuse you of being irresponsible. His
voice is raised, he's red in the face and he's pointing
his finger in your face. Now imagine what your self-
talk, at this point, might be! I suggest a 3-step
method for managing yourself:

Stop · Assess · Redirect
1) Stop, take a deep breath, ask yourself; "what am I
saying? Is it true?"
2) Assess – "Even if it's true, what's likely to happen
if I act on this current self-talk" and
3) Redirect by asking, "what do I want to have happen and what do I need to be saying in order to
effectively resolve this situation?"

Using the technique I described above, the process

would start by taking a deep breath, then assessing: "If I start yelling and defending myself, that will probably lead to an escalation of tension and conflict." The last step is to envision what you want, such as, "to maintain or enhance the relationship and clarify the concerns." I start by changing my self-talk to something like, "stay calm, I'm sure this is a mistake." "There has probably been a misunderstanding." "This person is certainly upset." "I'm sure I can help him through this frustration." "Listen and be open-minded." With this shift in self-talk, what might your presenting behavior likely be? Possibly more able to listen, stay calm, and ask clarifying questions and avoid an escalation of defensive behavior.

Reacting is always easier to do than responding.

You have no control over others ... you have only the ability to influence others through your own behavior.

One of the biggest barriers associated with managing yourself in relation to conflict, is learning to 'respond' to the other person versus 'reacting with hostility'.' If you use the skills outlined in this chapter, you can develop the ability to respond. Reacting is always easier to do than responding. Responding takes restraint and self-management—two behaviors that require a good deal of practice and are the most difficult to do when you need them the most. That's the value of the concept of self-talk and self-management. Sounds easy, but takes a lot of practice. Isn't as easy as it sounds but is well worth the effort of learning. You have no control over others ... you have only the ability to influence others through your own behavior.

Influence and Persuasion

In order to have any real impact on the outcome of an encounter, when two or more people are involved in a disagreement, it's critical to use not only the skills we previously mentioned, but also the behaviors and principles associated with influence and persuasion. Influence and persuasion take not only the ability to manage your presenting behavior, but also the ability to manage yourself—your self-talk. Developing these skills after years of indirect and passive behavior is as easy as losing weight—not easy at all, but it can be done. There are three steps in the process of influence and persuasion. They are:

Step one - listen actively

Step two - win a hearing

Step three - work to a common resolution.

Step One - Listen Actively

Listening actively is not something you can just read about and do; it's a skill that takes a great deal of practice. Given that truth, the steps you must follow in listening actively are to show others you understand: 1) that they have strong concerns and feelings, 2) what they feel strongly about, and 3) why they feel strongly about it. For example: A coworker comes to you with a complaint about a new project they've been assigned with concerns about the amount of time it will take and their fear that they won't be able to complete the project in that time frame. Your active listening response might sound something like: "I can see you are very concerned about this project and the short time frame in which you've been given to complete it, and fear it will affect upper management's perception of your abilities. Is that right?"

What's so magical about this practice? Remember as I stated before, "listening is a way of showing respect for another person and conversely, a lack of listening is a way of showing disrespect." How do you feel when you think you aren't being listened to? Listening is a powerful and influential skill. Lack of listening can contribute to reactive behaviors such as aggression, tension, anger as well as demotivation. When you listen for understanding you can begin to defuse tension and clear the way for problem solving.

When you listen for understanding you can begin to defuse tension and anger and clear the way for problem solving.

Step Two - Winning a Hearing

People will not generally listen to you if they feel you haven't listened to them.

People won't generally listen to you if they feel you haven't listened to them. You have to win a hearing by letting others know you've listened to their needs, concerns and thoughts. The first step you take to win a hearing is to prove you've listened to them by paraphrasing and referring back to their points; then you explain your own concern/feelings (backed up by relevant facts); and finally, you make your points assertively but stay friendly.

Prove you have listened to them by paraphrasing and referring back to their points.

Step Three - Work to a Common Resolution

Once all parties have had the opportunity to express their needs and concerns, it's time to work toward a common solution. The steps in working to a common solution are to:
1) ask for ideas,
2) build on ideas
3) offer your own ideas, and then
4) construct solutions from everyone's needs and ideas.

The above mentioned behaviors will lead to a meeting that has less tension, more creative energy and more commitment to the solutions. The demonstration of commitment can lead to a reduction in resistance, which often is present when the decision making process doesn't follow these steps.

All of this sounds pretty simple, even easy, but it isn't. The three most common difficulties in making this happen are:

1) These skills and behaviors require a great deal of mental effort. Most of us spend most of our time narrowly focused on the task in our encounters rather than on the quality of the interactions. This

lack of attention to the relationship undermines our efforts.

2) We haven't developed these skills over the years. Additionally, it takes a great deal of conscious effort to give up or 'unlearn' old habits and at the same time learn new skills.

3) The situations in which we need to apply the skills are often the ones where people feel under the most pressure, making them even more difficult to use.

Coming to a 'common solution' is a form of problem solving, so it's important to know there are actions that can undermine efforts in any problem solving process, these actions include: 1) interruptions, 2) contradictions and 3) demands/threats. These behaviors can lead to a lack of commitment to the resolution, escalation of the conflict and increase the potential for great harm to the relationship.

On the other hand, there are three actions that contribute to effective problem solving, and they are: 1) doubts, 2) questions and 3) information. The last 2 are obvious but the term 'doubt' may need some clarification. In this context the use of 'doubt' merely refers to ensuring your actions display a sense of openness to others' perspectives and points of view, as opposed to approaching the situation with certainty that your way is the only right way. Approaching with certainty can cause others to behave defensively, which can come in the form of rebelliousness, or immediate acquiescence. Whichever the response, ultimately, you won't find out what people really think.

Next we cover the skills associated with giving feedback and how it relates to managing conflict.

Feedback and Accountability

The ability to give and receive feedback is critical in any situation and certainly most critical in a conflict situation. When there's no feedback, there's no accountability. Feedback creates accountability. There are a variety of tips and models associated with feedback from the face-to-face confrontation to a mediation model. In this section we will be covering several types of feedback models that can be used in a variety of situations.

Why is feedback so hard? One of the key reasons is associated with fear. We may be fearful of the receiver's response or we may fear we are going to hurt someone's feelings. The key here is to remember, "method is everything." The way you give the feedback is often what causes a defensive response, so it's important to keep in mind the characteristics of effective feedback, which are to:

Ask for permission to give feedback.

(1) Ask for permission to give feedback. This may seem unusual, and it is. Most people, especially in close

relationships or at work, tend to take for granted that it's OK for them to give feedback—it's their job. Asking for permission to give feedback both prepares the recipient for the feedback, and it shows respect.

(2) Be descriptive and non-judgmental; describe what you see versus making judgments about what you see, for example, "You were rude in that meeting" (judgmental) versus "When you interrupted me during the meeting I felt as if you weren't interested in what I had to say" (descriptive).

Be descriptive and non-judgmental; describe what you see versus making judgments about what you see.

(3) Be specific; "You did a poor job on that report" (non-specific, too general) versus "I liked the opening remarks in the report and I suggest you put a summary at the end to bring full closure" (specific),

(4) Be focused on things which can change; "You look heavy in that pink suit" (the focus is on weight which cannot change at that moment) versus "a black, fitted suit will give a slimming effect—if that's important to you" (focus is on clothing which can be changed).

Additionally, in order to create an environment of accountability, it's important to get in the habit of asking for feedback and then thanking people for giving it to you. Remember, modeling is one of the most powerful forms of influence and instruction. When you effectively model giving and receiving feedback, you can greatly influence your environment.

Modeling is one of the most powerful forms of influence and instruction.

Another thing to remember with regard to feedback is to change the way you normally think about feedback. The term "feedback" often has the same negative connotations as conflict. We tend to associate feedback with being negative, delivering bad news, or hurting someone's feelings. If we start out with this type of belief about feedback, it's no wonder we don't want to give or receive it.

In truth, effective feedback is a way of showing concern for another person. Often the reason people fail in organizations, and relationships, is because they don't get effective feedback. When people are deprived of effective feedback, they may never know what it is that gets in the way of getting the results they want, so they continue with the same ineffective approaches or behaviors. If you begin to think about feedback as a way of showing concern and regard for another person, it's much easier to approach them and give them helpful feedback.

We all need feedback, whether it's in the form of praise to let us know that what we do is valued or as constructive feedback, which can help us become more effective. Feedback can be a powerful motivator and it is certainly the primary way to create accountability in any type of relationship.

We all need to hear good things about ourselves. It isn't enough to merely think good thoughts about others; it's very important to express those thoughts. We, too often, think that others should know how much we appreciate them—they don't. And besides, it's always good to hear. So get in the habit of expressing specifically what you like and appreciate about those with whom you work, live with and just encounter on a day-to-day basis. People derive energy from positive feedback (we all do!). Relationships can develop at a deeper level only when we are capable of being honest with one another—capable of giving effective feedback, both positive and constructive.

In order to improve our effectiveness at giving feedback, we must practice. Practice needs to include both positive and constructive forms of feedback, and in that practice you must use what you know about all the other issues associated with effective communication.

Next are examples of feedback that can create a defensive response, and a parallel example of feedback that can reduce the possibility of defensiveness. There are a lot of potential problems associated with the following statement: "You are always late getting information to me!" First, the statement starts with a "you" message, which can cause a defensive response from the beginning (we'll cover this 'barrier' in more detail in the next section). Another potential inflammatory word is "always." This word is a generalization and is usually inaccurate. The first thing the receiver of this message will likely do is defend herself by letting you know she "isn't always late getting the information to you" and she will let you know exactly how many times she got it to you on time.

In order to turn the above message into a more effective form of feedback and reduce the possibility of defensiveness, the speaker must first decide what he really needs from the individual to whom he is sending the message. In the example above, what the speaker really wants is information on time. To get that message across we might restate it by saying, "I noticed the information I need from you was late. What can be done to ensure I get this information on time?" This type of statement is assertive, specific and can lead to a problem-solving encounter.

In summary, the keys to creating an environment for effective feedback are to:
1) Ask for feedback for yourself,
2) Thank the person who gave you feedback,
3) Ask for permission to give feedback,
4) Be clear about what you want,
5) Avoid the common communication barriers,
6) Be assertive,
7) Be relevant,
8) Use what you know about influencing and persuading others, and of course,
9) Listen, listen, listen!

43

Empathy

Many years ago, in speaking with a fellow human resource/training and development professional, I mentioned something about empathy being a skill, and his response was to take offense. It seems he felt that to refer to the ability to show empathy as a skill was to minimize, trivialize or some how render it an insincere act. I don't think so. I think expressing empathy has to do more with awareness, desire and habit.

I think expressing empathy has to do more with awareness, desire and habit.

It's probably true that some people are incapable of showing empathy or maybe even of having empathy, I don't know about such things and that's probably a more appropriate topic for the psychological researchers and practitioners to address. One thing researchers have discovered is there are two ingredients that foster health and growth in any kind of relationship and those ingredients are (1) empathy and (2) acceptance.

Two ingredients that foster health and growth in any kind of relationship are (1) empathy and (2) acceptance.

Empathy is a powerful skill for showing that you have listened for understanding. When we think about how another person is feeling, and don't verbalize it, they don't get the benefit of knowing we have actually listened. That's why it's so important and powerful to express what you think they may be experiencing.

Empathy is a skill for developing understanding of another person's point-of-view about a situation and acknowledging his or her feelings about that situation. It's a way of showing concern and regard for 'the person' whether you agree with them or not. This is the big difference between empathy and sympathy. Empathy is a way of showing understanding; sympathy is a way of showing agreement. You don't have to agree to be empathetic.

Empathy is a way of showing understanding; sympathy is a way of showing agreement. You don't have to agree to be empathetic.

Whether you're interacting with a customer, an employee, a stranger or a friend, the ability to show empathy is a powerful gesture of respect and concern for the other person. Since empathy is a gesture of respect, concern, and caring, it's easy to understand the potential benefit of showing it in a variety of different situations. Many managers fail to show empathy because they're afraid that "if they give 'em an inch, they'll take a mile!" They fear it will show weakness on their part and the employee will take advantage of them. I find that couldn't be farther from the truth. You can be empathetic with an employee's difficult situation and still stay focused on problem solving. For example, let's say you have an employee (Jeff) who has come in late five days out of the past two weeks. You have to talk with him about this situation. When you confront him the following exchange takes place:

Empathy is a powerful gesture of respect and concern for the other person.

You can be empathetic with an employee's difficult situation and still stay focused on problem solving.

Wrong Way

Manager: "Jeff, I need to discuss something with you. I've noticed that you've been late five times out of the past two weeks. What's going on?"

Employee: "My son is in the hospital and I've tried to get by first thing in the morning so I can be there when he awakens."

Manager: "Well, Jeff, you know that when you're gone everyone else has to cover for you and that causes resentment. I need for you to be here on time."

How do you think Jeff is going to feel toward this manager? Will this encounter have improved or increased his loyalty, respect, motivation or productivity? I don't think so!

Better Way

Manager: "Jeff, I need to discuss something with you. I've noticed that you've been late five times out of the past two weeks. What's going on?"

Employee: "My son is in the hospital and I've tried to get by first thing in the morning so I can be there when he awakens."

Manager: "Jeff, I'm so sorry to hear this. What's the prognosis? How is he doing?"

Employee: "He's getting better. It was a pretty bad virus but I think we've about got it under control."

Manager: "That's good to hear, Jeff. What can we do to make sure that you get to spend the time you need with your son and ensure that things get covered here at work?"

The focus in the second scenario was on both the person and the task. Both aspects need to be addressed for the best results. Don't be afraid to show empathy—there are benefits for all parties involved.

Another type of situation in which empathy can be beneficial is with customers. Below is a service provider's remembrance of a difficult customer situation.

"I had heard about 'listening for understanding' for years, and last Tuesday I decided to do it with every person with whom I came in contact. I was very pleased with the results. For instance, one customer who regularly calls has always bothered me because she is so abrupt and impatient even when I tried to be friendly. On that Tuesday we had a pause while waiting for some information and we started talking personally. She mentioned that she was tired because she had been awakened at four a.m. by her mother who was suffering from Alzheimer's disease. Her mother was trying to get dressed and was putting a sweater on her legs like pants. My caller confessed how hard things had become because of her mother's disease. My impatience vanished. I began to understand why my caller was often irritable. It had nothing to do with me. It had to do with her family situation."

Another key to expressing empathy is to stay focused on the issue or concern and don't jump into problem solving right away. I use the following model to help me get started.

Empathy Model

Opening Phrase	Acknowledge the person and the feelings	Customer's view of the situation
"It sounds like"	you are concerned	about ...

Don't be afraid to acknowledge, through showing empathy, the concerns or feelings your employees or customers (friends or loved ones) may be experiencing; this behavior can create a more positive connection and strengthen your relationships.

Don't be afraid to acknowledge, through showing empathy, the concerns or feelings your employees or customers (friends or loved ones) may be experiencing; this behavior can create a more positive connection and strengthen your relationships.

Re-framing

The ability to re-frame is the ability to re-direct and change the tone of an encounter.

Another key skill associated with facilitating a conflict situation or mediating is that of re-framing. Good facilitators repeat what each party has to say after each step of the facilitation/mediation (see models in section 5). The ability to re-frame is the ability to redirect and change the tone of an encounter. This is a very useful skill!

Often times, in the course of facilitating or mediating a conflict, one of the parties may describe the other party's behavior in a very derogatory fashion. In order to keep the communication on track, a good facilitator/mediator will re-frame the derogatory statement to neutralize the effect.

Example

Original statement:

"He screwed me out of my money!"

Re-framed statement:

"I heard you say you felt cheated by the outcome of the trade."

Re-framing is a complementary skill to empathy. The value here is to manage the tone of the situation through re-framing derogatory or judgmental language and create a better environment in which to problem solve.

Questions

Occasionally, we find ourselves getting frustrated with people (customers or others) because we aren't getting the information we need to help us help them. Other times we may take action based on the information we did get, and end up with an outcome that's unsatisfactory to all parties. Some of us even blame the other party for not giving us accurate information in the first place.

I've discovered that often times the reason I don't get the information I need is because I've asked the question in an inappropriate format. The ability to ask appropriate and effective questions can mean the difference between success and failure in any endeavor whether it be determining the needs, concerns and wishes of a customer/client or a loved one or hiring the right person.

The ability to ask appropriate and effective questions can mean the difference between success and failure in any endeavor.

I first became aware of the importance of question formats when I became responsible for hiring and teaching others how to interview for hiring. The importance of developing the skill of questioning was again reinforced when I did, as one of my first consulting projects, a needs assessment with information systems professionals. One of the issues that sur-

I found most people tend to use only a couple of the question formats available to them, which has the potential of limiting the information they can surface.

faced as a key developmental need was related to the inability to get the type of information needed to provide their customers with the results they wanted. In my research and study of the use of questions, I found most people tend to use only a couple of the question formats available to them, which has the potential of limiting the information they can surface.

Following are five (5) question formats and their definitions.

Open Questions

•Open questions allow the other person to respond in any way s/he chooses.
example: "What can I do for you?"

•Use this format when you want the customer/person to respond freely, to get feelings, to start a conversation, and to expand on prior information.

Closed Questions

•A closed question limits the response a person can give.

•Often times the response is limited to choices like "either/or."
example: "Would you like black or white?"

•Other times the response is limited to "yes or no," or to a very short, specific answer.
example: "Would you like black?"
•When you ask a closed question, you're limiting or closing down the ways another person can answer you.
•Use this format when you need to get specific information quickly, when you want the customer/person to make a choice, and when you want to direct the conversation.

The difference between an open and a closed question is who controls the answer. When you ask a closed question, the questioner is controlling the possible responses. When you ask an open question the person to whom the question was directed is controlling the answer.

The difference between an open and a closed question is who controls the answer.

Fact-Finding Questions

•A fact-finding question is designed to get facts or information.
example: "When would you like us to deliver the heater?"

•A fact-finding question can be phrased in either a closed or an open format.
example: (open) "When would you like us to deliver the heater?"
example: (closed) "Can we deliver the heater on Wednesday?"

•Use this format when you want factual information to identify needs and expectations, and to get instructions.

Feeling-Finding Questions

•This format is designed to get you information about the customer's feelings.
•A feeling-finding question can also be open or closed.
example:(closed) "Would an afternoon delivery work for you?"
example:(open) "When would you prefer to have the heater delivered?"
•Use this format when you want to know about feelings, preferences, hopes and opinions. This tends to be the least used format and probably the most valuable. Most valuable because the things that get in the way of problem solving are generally related to

The things that get in the way of problem solving are generally related to unstated feelings, preferences and fears.

51

unstated feelings, preferences and fears.

Leading Questions

•This format telegraphs to the other person what you want them to say.
•It's almost always closed.
example: "You can accept this shipment after the delivery date, can't you?"
example: "You can work overtime, can't you?"

•Use this format when you don't want people to have a choice and be aware that you, as the questioner, are influencing the answer.

Becoming aware of what types of question formats you tend to use will require some real consciousness and discipline with a great potential payoff in terms of better results.

Section Four

Improving Your Awareness of the Eleven Common Communication Barriers

When we begin to see communication for the process it is, we can then begin to better manage that process. Communication is much like any other process, it is a little more difficult to observe, especially when we're in the process, than say a manufacturing process, but the more we know about communication and the barriers that can get in the way the more prepared we will be to take an appropriate action to reduce the impact of the barrier, or avoid it all together. Below is a list of common communication barriers that often contribute to an individual's defensive response. You'll recognize them because you probably use and hear them in everyday conversation.

I'll go through each of the barriers and give examples of how they may be presented, what the results may be, and how they might be avoided. It's important to note that these barriers often don't come by themselves — they come paired or even in multiples. They complement one another (an ugly complement).

Barriers

1) "Why"?

"Why" can put people on the defensive, because they feel they're being interrogated.

Definition - What's the barrier? It can put people on the defensive, because they feel they're being interrogated or that the questioner has little regard for their idea or position.

Unfurrow the brow and soften the tone.

Tone and non-verbals are what contribute to the word 'why' becoming a barrier. The way the word is delivered is the key. Unfurrow the brow and soften the tone. There's nothing inherently wrong with this word. It can become a problem when the tone accompanying it is harsh or when the speaker's non-verbal behaviors are misinterpreted.

Example: An employee, co-worker, child or spouse comes to you with a new idea on how to improve something and the response is something like, "Why would you want to take that approach?" If you start with "why" as your initial response, then you need to soften the tone of voice and delivery. Additionally, if what you really want is to know more about the suggestion, then ask for what you want, i.e: "Tell me more about how you think that will work?" Often times when we're curious or looking for understanding, we furrow our brow, which is a look of curiosity but can be interpreted as a frown or expression of dislike or disagreement.

2) Certainty versus Provisionalism (open mindedness)

Definition - What's the barrier? When approaching a

situation with certainty that "your way" is the "only right way," others will hold back from offering ideas since you give the impression you won't listen anyway vs. being open to others. Additionally, others may do worse things than hold back their ideas; they may rebel, resist or react as an unconscious response to the resentment they may feel from this perceived put down.

Whether it's with children, peers or the boss, "certainty" can quickly create defensive and reactive responses. This ineffective approach leaves little room for communication and problem solving. There's a difference between being confident about an option, and behaving in a way that conveys the message that you're certain your way is the only right way.

Example: I was called to help resolve some issues that had surfaced between three people working on a non-profit Board. The situation was described to me as follows; there was a great deal of tension between these three people, very little direct communication, insults, talking about one another instead of with one another, a lot of nasty e-mails. The Board President approached me because she saw that the continuation of this type of behavior would lead to factions, increased tensions among the non-combatants, possible loss of these or other Board members, possible loss of revenue and a great deal of energy would be diverted from the organization goals to these interpersonal issues.

The first step I took was to set up meetings with each of the individuals involved in the conflict. When I met with the first individual, she began to describe an encounter she had with one of the combatants. Her description was as follows: "She was determined to do things the way she wanted to do them instead of the right way." I asked her what was the right

> *"Certainty"* can *quickly create defensive and reactive responses.*

Being absolutely certain that "your way is the only right way" can alienate others, and it certainly leaves little room for options or problem solving.

way? Her response was "the way she learned from the National organization was the right way." Since the message the other person got was that there was only one right way, and her way was wrong, she resented this approach and reacted defensively. This is part of what caused an escalation in the conflict. Being absolutely certain that "your way is the only right way" can alienate others, and it certainly leaves little room for options or problem solving.

3) Intent vs. Impact

Definition - What's the barrier? The message that came across wasn't what the speaker intended.

Observation skills are critical here. If you say something to someone and the response you get is clearly inappropriate for the message you thought you sent, then you need to check and see if the message you thought you sent was what the other person heard.

Example: I might say to a co-worker, "You really did a great job on this report." My intention is to give a compliment; however, the person who heard this might be thinking, "Doesn't she think my other work has been good?" It is important to watch for signs that would suggest the person receiving the message might have interpreted it differently than you intended.

4) "But"

Definition - What's the barrier? This word minimizes everything that comes before it and focuses attention on the barriers that often follow it.

'And' is a building word; 'but' is a destructive word.

Use 'and' in place of 'but' as often as possible. 'And' is a building word; 'but' is a destructive word. 'And' can almost always be used in place of "but." When 'and' is used instead of 'but,' the statement becomes a building statement versus a destructive statement (building on versus putting down).

Example: "That's a good idea and in addition you might want to offer some thoughts about the costs associated with such a change." versus "That's a good idea, but it will cost too much."

5) Negative self-talk

Definition - What's the barrier? A method of undermining yourself or others when it can be controlled through redirection of your thoughts.

Negative self-talk is a method of undermining yourself or others when it can be controlled through redirection of your thoughts. Self-talk, whether it's negative or positive, can have a great effect on behavior, motivation and energy.

Self-talk, whether it's negative or positive, can have a great effect on behavior, motivation and energy.

Example: "I'm really not very good at speaking in front of people," versus "I don't speak very often in front of others, but this is a good opportunity to develop my skills." Both of these examples of self-talk can affect performance. Managing self-talk can help you either neutralize a negative message or even redirect to a positive message, thus influencing the use of your energies and affecting your behaviors.

Self-talk can also be directed toward others as well. For instance, you see a customer approaching you and it's someone with whom you've worked in the past. Your past experience with this individual is not a positive one, so your self-talk may sound like this: "Oh boy, her again! She is so difficult and pushy," versus "Here comes Jean. This may be a challenging and interesting experience."

6) Empathy versus Indifference

Definition - What's the barrier? Empathy is a means of showing concern and regard for another person vs. a lack of those behaviors.

The ability to show empathy is closely related to how effectively one listens. The use of empathy can also show respect and concern for others. Empathic behaviors can lead to strengthening of relationships and improving loyalty. The earlier section on skills shows examples of how empathy can enhance relationships and how the lack of it, indifference, can damage them.

7) Attaching motives

Definition - What's the barrier? When you attach motives to others behaviors, you assume you know why a person is thinking or taking a particular action without checking to see if the assumption is correct.

The only way you can know for sure what another person's behavior means is to ask.

The only way you can know for sure what another person's behavior means is to ask; otherwise, you're only assuming and your assumption may be incorrect. One thing is for sure; your assumption will affect the way you respond.

Example: A co-worker passes by my desk and doesn't speak, so I assume he's angry with me or that he intentionally snubbed me, when, in fact, the individual was deep in thought about a personal situation that occurred that morning. Any assumption we make about a person's behavior will affect the way we respond to that person.

8) Generalities versus Specifics

Definition - What's the barrier? Speaking in generalities, the use of broad general terms can lead to mis-interpretations and misunderstandings.

We tend to speak in generalities in our society and then wonder why there's so much miscommunication. It's particularly important to be specific when we're giving feedback, whether the feedback is positive or constructive.

We tend to speak in generalities in our society and then wonder why there is so much miscommunication.

Example: "You didn't do a very good job on your last report," versus "I noticed that on your last report you included a list of 'to do's' — that was a good addition. I'd also like to see you add a brief summary at the beginning of the report." Obviously, this approach to feedback would apply to personal relationships as well.

9) Judgmental versus Descriptive

Definition - What's the barrier? Using broad judgmental terms versus specific and descriptive terms. When one is judgmental, that tends to create a defensive response.

Descriptive feedback can decrease the possibility of defensiveness and leave room for problem solving.

Descriptive feedback can decrease the possibility of defensiveness and leave room for problem solving.

Example: "That was a stupid mistake," versus "I noticed that the figures in column one weren't added correctly. What can you do to ensure they are correct next time?"

10) "I" versus "You"

Definition - What is the barrier? The 'you' word tends to make people feel they are being blamed, which can create a defensive response.

Starting feedback with a "you" statement is like pointing a finger in the other person's face.

"You" statements tend to be blaming statements. Starting feedback with a "you" statement is like pointing a finger in the other person's face.

Example: "You did that wrong." Versus, "I noticed there's a mistake here."

11) Extreme terms

Definition - What's the barrier? These are terms that are general, non-specific and often inaccurate, such as "always and never."

Example: "You're always late to staff meeting." The first thing the person receiving this type of feedback is likely to do is defend themselves and list all the times they weren't late. These statements are generalities and usually inaccurate, thus leading to a defensive response.

Words are like diamonds delivered in a dump truck.

Words, in and of themselves, are neutral. We as speakers and listeners provide the meaning. Words are like diamonds delivered in a dump truck and we are the dump trucks. Additionally, tone of voice and non-verbal behaviors contribute to the interpretation of any statement, so awareness of non-verbal behavior and tone are critical in managing your effectiveness. I've included below parts of a poem by Charles Harper Webb; a prize-winning poet who has captured the power of this aspect of communication in his poem entitled "Tone of Voice" from his book entitled *Liver*:

> *"State your name" from lawyers' lips can mean, "You lie!"*
> *Tone leaks the truth despite our best efforts to hide.*

In most all endeavors in life, method is the key to effectiveness. The same is true for communication. Communication is a process; it can be improved, tweaked, mastered, manipulated and very intentional. The information we've covered in this section is the complement to the processes you'll be reading about in the next section. It takes both process knowledge (the how to) and content knowledge (the what) to become a more skillful and effective communicator.

Knowing about and understanding different models and processes for conflict management and problem solving will allow you more options, flexibility and freedom in your relationships. Following, in Section Five, I've listed several models I use in my work as resources for you.

It takes both process knowledge (the how to) and content knowledge (the what) to become a more skillful and effective communicator.

Section Five

Models for Conflict Management and Problem Solving

The model you use to help manage conflict or problem solve will depend on the type of conflict or problem with which you're faced. We'll look at models ranging from mediation to one-on-one confrontation. Below is a model for managing conflict in which a facilitator is used. On the left side of the page are the steps, and listed on the right are the specific skills it takes to manage each of the steps. This model might be used when two parties are in conflict, can't seem to resolve it, and need the help of a third party. In an organization this conflict might be between peers or a boss and employee. It might be between people in the same department or in different departments. The primary characteristic is that these individuals have not been able to solve the problem on their own and need some help. The third party may be a supervisor, a human resource representative or an individual who has been contracted from outside of the company. Whichever the choice, the key is that the facilitator has experience and ability in managing such a process.

The first step in this process is for the facilitator to meet individually with each person who's involved in the conflict. This is done for a variety of reasons: 1) to help determine the issues; 2) for the facilitator to begin to establish a trusting relationship with both parties; and most importantly, 3) to discover if each person has the desire and commitment to resolve the conflict. If the desire to resolve or commitment isn't there, then the conflict can't be resolved. Once the facilitator has determined that these characteristics are there, they will then begin with the steps listed immediately following:

If the commitment isn't there, then the conflict can't be resolved.

Action	Skills/ Characteristics
Step 1: Set the climate; make sure everyone has an appropriate amount of time available. State your intentions, the purpose of the meeting and explain the process. If you're facilitating a conflict between two people, you will have spoken with both individually prior to this session.	• Specificity • Confidence • Descriptive • Problem solving •Facilitation

Step 2: Clearly state your concern, describe the actual behavior/performance and the desired performance/behavior. Explain why it's a concern/problem and the extent to which it's affecting work performance (theirs and others). "The angry encounters which have occurred periodically between you and David have created a situation in which others in the organization feel they must take sides. That causes discomfort and moves attention away from work. It also creates a very tense atmosphere." (use specific examples of decreased work performance when possible, i.e., missed deadlines)	• Specificity • Observation • Descriptive • "I" messages
Step 3: Establish your expectations and belief that the conflict is probably the result of a misunderstanding and can be resolved. "I believe this situation can be cleared up if we choose to do so. I expect all of us will work at resolving this issue."	• Supportive • Provisional
Step 4: Clearly identify the objectives of the meeting and stay focused on those objectives, i.e. "We are here to find out specifically what is troubling each of you so that you can develop a more effective and enjoyable working relationship."	• Problem solving • Objectivity

Step 5: Help defuse anger by acknow-ledging feelings that may exist. "I can't be sure how either of you feel, but when I've experienced situations like this in the past, I've felt angry, hurt and confused. That's normal."	• Active listening • Empathy
Step 6: Establish the rules for exchanging information. "I would like for both of you to identify each behavior (specifically what it is that the other person is doing or saying) and how you feel about that behavior. Then list what behavior you would like to see in place and why. Name calling is not okay."	• Problem solving • Confidence • Facilitation
Step 7: Facilitate negotation with each person on the ideal behavior and get commitment.	• Listening • Facilitation • Observation
Step 8: Set a follow-up date to check progress. "Let's meet back here in my office next Friday the 11th at 4:00. Will that work for both of you?	

As the facilitator of this type of process you want to keep in mind the following:

• The process should be visible (use a flipchart if possible).

• There is probably a great deal of anger between the people involved. Let people vent and then refocus.

• There will be many attempts to sidetrack. Stay focused on behaviors, feelings and desired outcome.

• Express to each person the fact that they will initially feel uncomfortable trying new behaviors. That's normal.

• Ask if there's anything you can do to help.

• To maintain your balance, remember that conflict is a result of caring. Conflict can lead to creative alternatives and increased energy.

One of the most important acts associated with this or any other conflict resolution model is follow-up.

Using a flip chart makes the process visible, creates documentation and keeps energy focused forward. One of the most important acts associated with this or any other conflict resolution model is follow-up. Looking ahead to the follow-up session helps people stay focused, and it underscores the importance of the process and work that has been done. When there is no follow-up after any type of performance feedback, the unintended message you are sending is that "this really isn't very important."

The next model is the more common. It's a one-to-one model of feedback or confrontation. This may take place between peers or a boss/employee-type situation, or on a more personal level, it could take place between parent/child, spouses or significant others.

Keep in mind the issues associated with assertiveness such as staying focused on what is relevant. Before you go into any confrontation situation be aware of your self-talk. That is how you will most effectively manage your own behavior, which will lead to a more effective outcome. The face-to-face, one-to-one model follows for your review.

Feedback Model

Step 1: Raise the issue: "I'm concerned about_____
_____.

Step 2: Describe the specifics (avoid accusations and defensiveness by using "I" statements) "When _____happens, the result is
_____
_____
and I feel_____.

a) Encourage the other person to discuss how he or she sees the situation by using open-ended questions.
"How do you see the situation?"
"Please share your thoughts with me..."
"What could be causing this result?"

b) Summarize the other person's remarks to ensure that you understand his perception.
"So you see it as..."
"From your perspective it looks like..."

Step 3: Request a Change in Behavior from actual to desired.

a) Mutually discuss ways of eliminating the problem.
   "In the future, how can we.."
   "How do you think this could have been avoided?"

b) Actively seek the other person's ideas and suggestions. Encourage the other person to set targets for him/herself.

c) Make suggestions, if you have any.
   "Here's what I would suggest..."

Step 4: Agree on a plan of action.

a) Summarize what's been discussed and confirm your commitment. Show enthusiasm for the plans made. Be positive. "Ok, so I'll......and you'll......"

b) Give the other person an opportunity to make any final suggestions.
   "Anything else we should discuss?"

c) Set a time and place for evaluation.
   "Let's plan on meeting again in 2 weeks, same day and time to discuss progress?"

d) Close the discussion on a friendly, upbeat note.
   "I feel better now that we've discussed this, and I hope you do, too."

Step 5: Follow-up.

a) If the situation warrants it, you may want to keep a written record of the discussion and agreement.

b) Evaluate how you handled the discussion and what you would do differently in the future.

c) Set up a system for follow through (i.e. write the dates in your calendar, update your personnel files, etc.)

d) Assist the other person in making the changes you have agreed upon.

The next model is the traditional mediation model. The mediation model is a facilitated model very similar to the first model we covered. The mediator should be someone who is certified or practiced in mediation. Again, this could be a situation in which the conflict is over anything imaginable and it could be between peers, supervisor/employee, children/parents, etc.

The way the mediation model differs from the first model is that it can be used effectively even when the mediator doesn't know the parties involved and doesn't necessarily meet with them before the session. It is important for the mediator to explain clearly, to the participants in the mediation (conflict) session, the role of the mediator. That role includes:

1) assisting the parties in communicating
2) assisting the parties in discovering the best solution to meet both their needs
3) keeping the process on track and the participants focused. The mediator's role is not to solve the problems or make suggestions, the solutions must come from the participants.

A Mediation Model

Step 1

The mediator will introduce him/herself to each party (if they're unknown to those parties) and establish who will go first. This could be done by the toss of a coin or by volunteering. Often times this model is used with strangers and that's the reason the introduction is included. When used internally by a supervisor or manager this step will be used primarily to clarify purpose and expectations, i.e., "we 're here to determine a resolution suitable to both parties."

Step 2

The mediator will explain the process as follows:
• Each person will be asked to explain the situation from his /her perspective. We may go back to each person to surface more information, if necessary.

The mediator will repeat back what they understood the party to say after they complete their explanation.
• Each person will be asked to come up with ideas for a solution/s and build on each other's ideas until an agreement is reached. Again, the mediator will repeat the suggestion/s and ask the other party if they can agree to any of the suggestions or what additional suggestions they might have for resolution.

Step 3
The mediator will ask each party to agree to the following rules:
• when one party is speaking, the other party is to remain silent and make no distracting noises or comments.
• each party will direct their observations and solutions to the mediator and not to one another.
• no name calling or distracting behavior.

Step 4
• Start the process.

Step 5
• Document the agreed upon solution/s.

The process of mediation is one in which the primary purpose is to leave ownership of the solution in the hands of the parties who need mediation. People always try harder to make a solution work if it's of their own making. The mediator is there solely to assist in managing communication.

The next model is a scientific problem- solving model that can be used quite effectively in dealing with people issues as well. It's called "Gap Analysis."

Gap Analysis

This process can be used on a one-to-one basis or one to many. The facilitator may be a supervisor who's problem solving with an employee who has an absenteeism problem, or it may be as a facilitator working with a group to address an issue/s affecting them.

The ability to be specific and descriptive is critical to using this model. You'll see below why I've stressed specificity.

Step 1: Set the stage by explaining to the party/ies involved that you are coming together to identify, discuss and address an issue/s of concern to both of them.

Step 2: Describe to the individual (employee, etc.) exactly what it is you'd like to see, 'ideal' behavior or outcomes. Then describe what you do see, 'actual' behavior or outcomes.

Step 3: Ask the individuals what they can do, specifically, to move from actual to ideal. The key here is related to getting specifics from the individual being asked to change. For instance a response of, "I'll try harder," isn't specific and won't do. You would ask a follow-up question such as, "specifically what will you do to try harder?" A more graphic interpretation of this model is listed below.

ACTUAL  IDEAL

<u>What, specifically, are you going to do to close the Gap between Ideal and Actual behaviors/actions?</u>

This model is surprisingly simple and surprisingly effective. The same process can work with group problem solving; the difference will be in asking the group to brainstorm 'ideal' and 'actual' and then asking them to identify the steps to remove the 'Gap.' All of the models we've discussed are simple to use but they aren't easy; ease will come with practice!

Section Six

Closing

More often than not, when I intervene in a conflict situation between two or more people, invariably the individuals involved are reacting to one another because they're not getting their needs met. For example, some individuals may have a need to be acknowledged for the contributions they're making to a situation or relationship. Since they feel their contributions are being overlooked, they may "act out" in order to get the recognition they desire. As much as we like to deny it, believe it or not, adults do 'act out.' Additionally, labeling adult behavior as childish creates another barrier to solving the problem because that label minimizes and trivializes what is not childish behavior but is human behavior.

Labeling adult behavior as childish creates another barrier to solving the problem because that label minimizes and trivializes what's not childish behavior but is human behavior.

73

Acting out tends to bring an escalation of animosity and tension versus getting what the individuals really want, getting their needs met. Another dynamic, which is often present in conflict situations, is the belief on the part of one or both of the people that their way is the only right way. "Being right" can get in the way of being creative.

"Being right" can get in the way of being creative.

If all of us were good at identifying and expressing our needs, then we wouldn't have this type of problem. But many of us aren't good at expressing our needs so we continue to feel unrecognized or unfulfilled and never learn a more effective way to get our needs met. Additionally, you can't argue a person out of their needs and concerns; you must help them address and overcome them.

You can't argue a person out of their needs and concerns; you must help them address and overcome them.

You may not find resolution to each situation every time a conflict surfaces in your life. Sometimes relationships will end or change dramatically because an effective resolution didn't come about, but as you continue to develop the kinds of skills we've covered in the book, you'll feel more confident in your ability to get what you want and need from relationships and help others to get what they need as well.

We've discussed many tools for helping you become more effective with communication and managing conflict. It's important to think about what can get in the way of using what you've learned. Too often the biggest reasons or excuses we make to ourselves are that "No one else will do it," "It might not work," "It might backfire," or "It won't make any difference anyway." The key to making a difference in the quality of your own life is to remember that change doesn't just begin with you — in fact, you're the only one who can truly make it happen (or keep it from happening)!

1) Our actions subtly (or overtly) influence others and norms (accepted behaviors) are created. "I guess that's the appropriate behavior here (in this relationship)." Then...

2) These norms begin to give shape to and define the environment. More individuals are influenced. "It seems that behavior is expected here (in this relationship)!" Then...

3) The environment now reinforces these individual behaviors. "That's the way we do things here (in this relationship)!" Then...

4) The cycle continues, and suddenly you have a "Corporate (departmental or home) Culture". "It's too bad it has to be this way! (If only they would...")

We face dozens of opportunities every day to help change the norms or to remain "victims" of the environment or situation. The choice is always our own. To change the culture or dynamics in a relationship, you have to change the environment. To change the environment, you have to change the norms. To change the norms, you have to change individual behaviors.

Real change will not occur because of a few BIG decisions from the top, if we're referring to an organization, (though they may help). It will only come from the hundreds of little decisions each of us make every day. Your choices, no matter how small, will make a difference. It starts with YOU!

Culture is created and defined by the way we choose to deal with the issues and each other. As individual behaviors change, so does the "culture." Too often people see themselves as "victims" of "the way things are." Now you have the information and knowledge to accept the challenge, take ownership and create the change you desire or be the change you wish to see.

Culture is created and defined by the individuals and the way we choose to deal with the issues and each other.

Additionally, in order to become more effective with

managing conflict, practicing the skills and using the information we've covered will cause you to face the issues associated with change. It's difficult to change behaviors you have been using for a lifetime. If your approach to conflict has been "to avoid," I can guarantee it will be difficult to practice being assertive and specific when those aren't the behaviors with which you've felt comfortable in the past.

Change is simple....
It's just not easy!

Change is simple. ... It's just not easy! A change in behavior is hard because it puts us in new situations that are initially uncomfortable. For that reason we may tend to use avoidance behavior so we don't have to feel this discomfort. We all go through transitional steps when we practice new behaviors. We feel uncomfortable with these behaviors until, finally, the practice pays off. We now own the behaviors and feel comfortable using them.

The act of moving from one behavior, or one state or condition, is a transition/change and if we stop because of the discomfort of the change, we tend to go back to that comfortable place (old behavior)....
if we can.

How we respond to transitions in our lives is critical to our success with regard to how we move through the challenges that confront us on a daily basis. The act of moving from one behavior, or one state or condition, is a transition/change and if we stop because of the discomfort of the change, we tend to go back to that comfortable place (old behavior) ... if we can.

This intellectual understanding was translated through a practical experience for me one winter when I was dealing with very icy conditions. We had a big ice storm. All the streets were treacherous and drivers were being very cautious. As the ice began to thaw the effect it had on my approach to driving was a reflection of how most of us feel when we go through a transition in our lives. The side streets were still treacherous but, most of the main roads were relatively passable except for a few icy spots. The highways were primarily clear except for snow and ice accumulated on the shoulders. I found myself being in a more tense state than I was when all the roads were the same, because I didn't know what to expect. People around me were driving with less caution, some with little regard for the conditions at all. That period when there's very little certainty or when you have little ability to predict outcomes based on familiar circumstances, is what all transitions feel like. Once we make it through that period we then start feeling more comfortable with the situation, stress decreases - we've made it to the other side of the transition.

When people have such great fear of going through change (transitions) and instead hang on to what's familiar (the past), they often find that a change will occur anyway, but it will no longer be on their terms. Then they become a victim of their situation. Having an illusion of control by hanging on to the past can ultimately lead to a greater loss of opportunity than the short term loss of comfort, which is part of any transition period.

Continued resistance to change can mean that the change will happen anyway, but the terms will be dictated by someone else or by circumstances. You can take the risk of trying to respond to conflict differently than you have in the past, or you can take the risk of doing the same thing you've always done. Just remember that either way is a risk.

Best wishes,
Barbara Bannon

That period when there is very little certainty or when you have little ability to predict outcomes based on familiar circumstances, is what all transitions feel like.

Continued resistance to change can mean that the change will happen anyway, but the terms will be dictated by someone else or by circumstances.

Section Seven
About the Author

Barbara Bannon is the principal consultant of Human Resource Investments (HRI), a consulting and organization development company specializing in management and employee development. Her practice places special emphasis on conflict management, mediation, team-building and customer service training. She founded HRI in February of 1990 after resigning from MAPCO, a Fortune 500 company, where she held the position of Manager of Employee Relations and Training.

Barbara has been in the field of Human Resources and Training and Development for over twenty-five years. She is an adjunct professor in the Spears School of Business at Oklahoma State University, teaching Diversity in the Workplace, where she has received recognition as an Outstanding Professor.

Barbara is a certified mediator through the Supreme Court of Oklahoma and has conducted hundreds of civil and divorce mediations as well as workplace mediations and conflict resolutions.

Additionally, she is a member and past president of the American Society for Training and Development (ASTD) and has been awarded the Outstanding Contributor Award in the field of Training and Development from ASTD. She has also served on the board of the Tulsa Area Human Resource Association where she has been nominated, by her clients/peers, three times for the Excellence Award in Human Resource Practices. She's past president of the Board of Resonance (a support center for women and their families), and was nominated by the Resonance staff for the Paragon Award for Excellence in

Community Leadership. She's served on many other boards and has been very active in her city and state. For more information about Barbara and HRI, you can go to her website: **humanresourceinvestments.com**